BY KATHRYN WALTON

VOL. I *From Past to President* 1801

THOMAS JEFFERSON

Please visit our website, www.enslow.com. For a free color catalog of all our high-quality books, call toll free 1-800-398-2504 or fax 1-877-980-4454.

Cataloging-in-Publication Data

Names: Walton, Kathryn, 1993-.
Title: Thomas Jefferson / Kathryn Walton.
Description: Buffalo, NY : Enslow Publishing, 2025. | Series: From past to president | Includes glossary and index.
Identifiers: ISBN 9781978542457 (pbk.) | ISBN 9781978542464 (library bound) | ISBN 9781978542471 (ebook)
Subjects: LCSH: E332.79 W36 2025
Classification: LCC W345 2025 | DDC 973.4'6092

Published in 2025 by
Enslow Publishing
2544 Clinton Street
Buffalo, NY 14224

Copyright © 2025 Enslow Publishing

Portions of this work were originally authored by Gillian Gosman and published as *Thomas Jefferson*. All new material in this edition is authored by Kathryn Walton.

Designer: Claire Zimmermann
Editor: Natalie Humphrey

Photo credits: Cover (Thomas Jefferson portrait), pp. 13, 18, 19 courtesy of the Library of Congress; cover (Monticello photo) eurobanks /Shutterstock.com; cover (quill illustration), p. 12 Istry Istry /Shutterstock.com; cover (ink splotch) Plateresca/Shutterstock.com; cover (signature) Appletons'_Thomas_Jefferson_Signature.jpg/Wikimedia Commons; cover (newspaper clipping), p. 12 STILLFX/Shutterstock.com; cover (author name scrap), series art (caption background) Robyn Mackenzie/Shutterstock.com; series art (purple paper background) OLeksiiTooz/Shutterstock.com; cover (newspaper text background at lower left) MaryValery/Shutterstock.com; series art (newspaper text background) TanyaFox/Shutterstock; series art (More to Learn antique tag) Mega Pixel/Shutterstock.com; pp. 5, 6, 11, 15, 19 (ripped blank newspaper piece) STILLFX/Shutterstock.com; p. 5 Official_Presidential_portrait_of_Thomas_Jefferson_(by_Rembrandt_Peale,_1800)_(cropped).jpg/Wikimedia Commons; p. 6 William_and_Mary_College_before_the_fire_of_1859.jpg/Wikimedia Commons; p. 7 OJUP/Shutterstock.com; p. 9 Anthony George Visuals/Shutterstock.com; p. 11 Allan_Ramsay_-_King_George_III_in_coronation_robes_-_Google_Art_Project.jpg/Wikimedia Commons; p. 15 Mather_Brown_-_Thomas_Jefferson_-_Google_Art_Project_(cropped).jpg/Wikimedia Commons; p. 17 courtesy of the New York Public Library.

Some of the images in this book illustrate individuals who are models. The depictions do not imply actual situations or events.

All rights reserved. No part of this book may be reproduced in any form without permission in writing from the publisher, except by a reviewer.

Printed in the United States of America

CPSIA compliance information: Batch #CWENS25: For further information contact Enslow Publishing at 1-800-398-2504.

CONTENTS

President Thomas Jefferson .4

Growing Up in Virginia 6

Monticello 8

Working Hard 10

The Declaration of Independence 12

Governing Virginia 14

Vice President Jefferson 16

Finally President .18

Remembering Jefferson 20

President Jefferson's Timeline 21

Glossary 22

For More Information 23

Index 24

Words in the glossary appear in **bold** type the first time they are used in the text.

PRESIDENT
THOMAS JEFFERSON

Thomas Jefferson was known as a great thinker. He is remembered as an important writer too. During his lifetime, Jefferson wrote the Declaration of Independence and many letters. He even wrote a short book about his life!

Jefferson had many sides, some of which were at odds with themselves. While he believed strongly in freedom, he also kept more **enslaved** people than any other president. To understand why, we first need to go back to Jefferson's youth in Shadwell, Virginia.

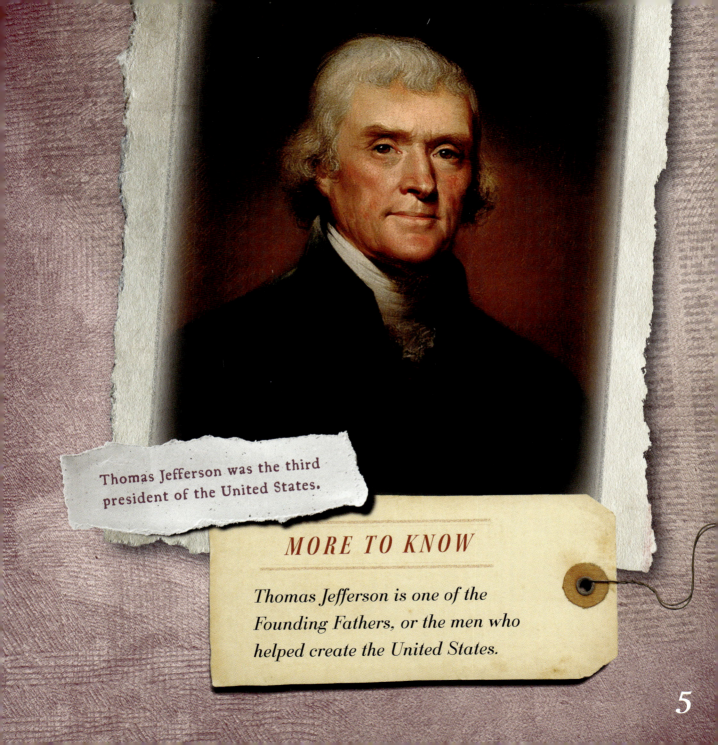

Thomas Jefferson was the third president of the United States.

MORE TO KNOW

Thomas Jefferson is one of the Founding Fathers, or the men who helped create the United States.

GROWING UP IN VIRGINIA

Thomas Jefferson was born on April 13, 1743. His family owned a plantation, or a large farm. Jefferson's father died when Jefferson was 14 years old. He left Jefferson his land and the enslaved people living there.

Jefferson loved learning. He went to the College of William and Mary at the age of 16. People said that Jefferson would study for 15 hours a day. He would play the violin for many hours after he finished studying.

College of William and Mary

MORE TO KNOW

Thomas Jefferson had six sisters and one brother. He was the eldest son.

Jefferson's family was wealthy. Much of their money came from the sale of crops grown in fields worked by enslaved people.

MONTICELLO

Jefferson graduated from the College of William and Mary in 1762. After he graduated, he studied law under the **lawyer** George Wythe. In 1767, Jefferson began working as a lawyer himself.

In the following year, Jefferson began work on Monticello. Monticello was a large home and plantation built on the land his father left him. Jefferson continued adding to Monticello throughout his life. The home wouldn't be finished until 1809.

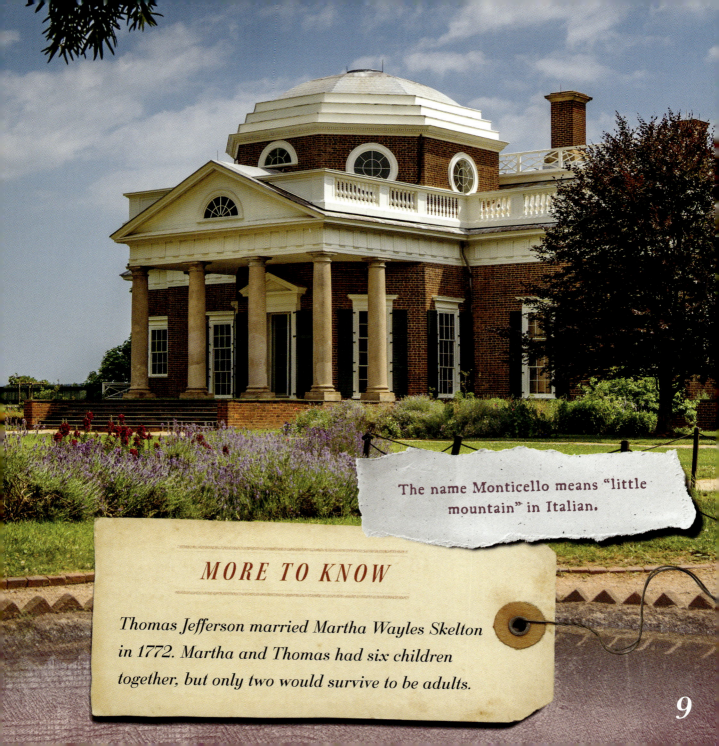

The name Monticello means "little mountain" in Italian.

MORE TO KNOW

Thomas Jefferson married Martha Wayles Skelton in 1772. Martha and Thomas had six children together, but only two would survive to be adults.

WORKING HARD

Jefferson began serving in the Virginia House of Burgesses in 1769. This was the Virginia colony's government. Jefferson was an important member and often wrote or worked on **committees**.

By the 1760s and the 1770s, many colonists spoke about breaking free from British rule. Jefferson believed it was unfair that the colonists did not have **representatives** to speak for them in the British government. But Great Britain wouldn't give up the colonies without a fight.

King George III, the British ruler at this time, was against freedom for the colonies.

MORE TO KNOW

Jefferson was part of the Secret Committee of **Correspondence**. This committee worked with other European countries to gather support for American freedom.

THE DECLARATION OF INDEPENDENCE

In 1775, the **American Revolution** began. Jefferson was chosen to be a representative in the Second Continental Congress, the governing body of the colonies at the time. Jefferson was in his early 30s when he joined the Second Continental Congress.

MORE TO KNOW

The Declaration of Independence stated all the ways Jefferson believed the British had wronged the colonies.

12

The Continental Congress asked Jefferson to write why they wanted independence from Great Britain. Jefferson's **document** was called the Declaration of Independence. The Congress approved the declaration on July 4, 1776.

Fifty-six members of the Continental Congress signed the Declaration of Independence.

GOVERNING
VIRGINIA

In 1779, Jefferson became the governor of Virginia. The colonies were still fighting the British at this time, and Jefferson had to work hard to keep Virginia safe. He served two terms as governor.

Jefferson's wife wouldn't live to see the end of the war. On September 6, 1781, Martha Jefferson died. The American Revolution went on for another two years.

MORE TO KNOW

After his wife died, Jefferson shut himself in his room for three weeks. When he finally came out, he went to France as a **diplomat**.

Jefferson would continue living and working in France for many years.

VICE PRESIDENT
JEFFERSON

In Jefferson's time, presidential **candidates** didn't run for office with a vice presidential candidate. Instead, the candidate with the most votes in the **Electoral College** became president. The candidate with the second-highest number of votes became the vice president.

In 1796, Jefferson ran for president and lost. He became John Adams' vice president, even though Jefferson and Adams were from different political parties. They often disagreed about how the government should be run.

MORE TO KNOW

A political party is a group of people with similar beliefs about how government should be run who try to win elections together.

THOMAS JEFFERSON,
Vice President of the U.S.

In a letter, Jefferson said, "The second office of this government is honorable and easy."

FINALLY PRESIDENT

Jefferson ran for president again in 1800. This time, the election ended in a tie between Jefferson and Aaron Burr. The House of Representatives had to pick the winner. They voted 36 times before agreeing that Jefferson would be the president and Burr would be the vice president.

During Jefferson's presidency, the United States bought the Louisiana Territory from France in 1803. Jefferson sent explorers to map the new territory and displayed some of what they found at the White House.

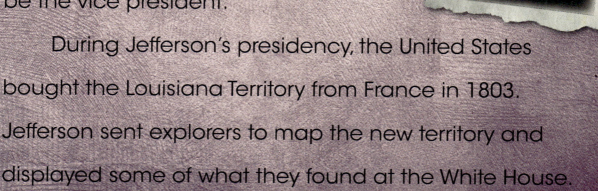

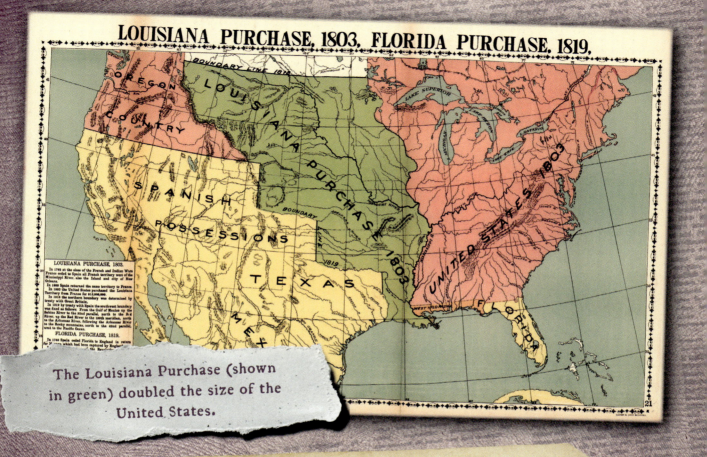

The Louisiana Purchase (shown in green) doubled the size of the United States.

MORE TO KNOW

The explorers Meriwether Lewis and William Clark brought back tools, animal skins, plants, and more from their travels in the Louisiana Territory.

19

REMEMBERING JEFFERSON

Jefferson was reelected in 1804. His second term wasn't as successful as his first. He started an **embargo** on goods from Europe to stay out of European politics. This embargo hurt Americans and didn't work well.

In 1809, Jefferson returned home to Monticello. He would live the rest of his life farming, writing, and inventing. On July 4, 1826, exactly 50 years after the Declaration of Independence was signed, Thomas Jefferson died. He was 83.

MORE TO KNOW

Jefferson made it illegal to bring more enslaved people into the country. Despite doing this, he only freed seven of his own enslaved people.

PRESIDENT JEFFERSON'S TIMELINE

APRIL 13, 1743

Thomas Jefferson is born in Virginia.

1760

Jefferson starts attending the College of William and Mary.

1767

He begins work as a lawyer.

1769

Jefferson begins serving in the Virginia House of Burgesses.

1772

He and Martha are married.

1775

Jefferson represents Virginia at the Second Continental Congress.

1776

He writes the Declaration of Independence.

1779

Jefferson becomes governor of Virginia.

1797

Jefferson becomes the vice president of the United States.

1801

Jefferson becomes president of the United States for the first time.

1803

Jefferson purchases the Louisiana Territory from France.

1805

Jefferson becomes the president of the United States the second time.

JULY 4, 1826

Jefferson dies at 83.

GLOSSARY

American Revolution: The war in which the American colonies won their freedom from Great Britain.

candidate: Someone who wants to serve in or be elected to a government office.

committee: A group of people who are chosen to do a certain job together.

correspondence: All the emails, letters, and more that a person, group, or company sends and receives.

diplomat: A person who is skilled at talks between nations.

document: A formal piece of writing.

Electoral College: A group of people who pick the president based on who gets the most votes in their states.

embargo: A country banning trade with another country.

enslaved: Having to do with being owned by another person and forced to work without pay.

lawyer: Someone whose job it is to help people with their questions and problems with the law.

representative: A member of a lawmaking body who acts for voters.

FOR MORE INFORMATION

BOOKS

Knopp, Ezra E. *Myths and Facts About Thomas Jefferson.* Buffalo, NY: PowerKids Press, 2024.

London, Martha. *Thomas Jefferson.* Lake Elmo, MN: Focus Readers, 2023.

WEBSITES

National Geographic Kids: Thomas Jefferson
https://kids.nationalgeographic.com/history/article/thomas-jefferson
Learn more about Thomas Jefferson's life and the work he did as president.

Monticello
www.monticello.org/
Take a virtual tour of Monticello or plan a visit to Thomas Jefferson's historic home!

Publisher's note to educators and parents: Our editors have carefully reviewed these websites to ensure that they are suitable for students. Many websites change frequently, however, and we cannot guarantee that a site's future contents will continue to meet our high standards of quality and educational value. Be advised that students should be closely supervised whenever they access the internet.

INDEX

Adams, John, 16

birthday, 6

children, 9

college, 6, 8, 21

death, 20, 21

Declaration of Independence, 4, 12, 13, 21

enslaved people, 4, 6, 7, 20

father, 6, 8

Founding Fathers, 5

France, 14, 15, 18, 21

governor, 14, 21

Great Britain, 10, 13

home, 8, 20

Louisiana Territory, 18, 21

plantation, 6, 8

political party, 16, 17

second term, 20

Shadwell, Virginia, 4

siblings, 7

Skelton, Martha Wayles, 9, 14, 21

studying, 6

vice presidency, 16, 21

violin, 6

Virginia House of Burgesses, 10, 21

Wythe, George, 8